2021
LOS ANGELES
Restaurants

The Food Enthusiast's Long Weekend Guide

Andrew Delaplaine

GET 3 FREE NOVELS
Like political thrillers?
See next page to download 3 FREE page-turning
novels—no strings attached.

Andrew Delaplaine is the Food Enthusiast.
When he's not playing tennis,
he dines anonymously
at the Publisher's expense.

WANT 3 **FREE** THRILLERS?

Why, of course you do!
If you like these writers--
Vince Flynn, Brad Thor, Tom Clancy, James Patterson, David Baldacci, John Grisham, Brad Meltzer, Daniel Silva, Don DeLillo
If you like these TV series –
House of Cards, Scandal, West Wing, The Good Wife, Madam Secretary, Designated Survivor

You'll love the **unputdownable** series about Jack Houston St. Clair, with political intrigue, romance, and loads of action and suspense.

Besides writing travel books, I've written political thrillers for many years that have delighted hundreds of thousands of readers. I want to introduce you to my work!
Send me an email and I'll send you a link where you can download the first 3 books in my bestselling series, absolutely FREE.
Mention **this book** when you email me.
andrewdelaplaine@mac.com

Copyright © by Gramercy Park Press - All rights reserved.
Cover photo by Dave Herring on Unsplash

Los Angeles

The Food Enthusiast's
Long Weekend Guide

Table of Contents

Chapter 1
BEVERLY HILLS – 5
Westwood – Culver City – Century City – Brentwood

Chapter 2
WEST HOLLYWOOD & HOLLYWOOD – 25

Chapter 3
DOWNTOWN – 50
Koreatown – Chinatown – Wilshire – Little Tokyo
La Brea – East Hollywood – Silver Lake

Chapter 4
SANTA MONICA & VENICE – 93

Chapter 5
NIGHTLIFE – 111

INDEX – 113

Chapter 1
BEVERLY HILLS
Westwood – Culver City – Century City – Brentwood

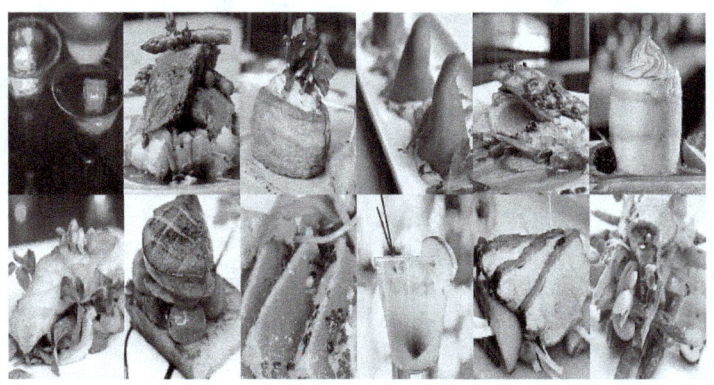

AMICI
469 N. Doheny Dr., Beverly Hills: 310-274-8141
www.cafeamicibh.com
CUISINE: Italian
DRINKS: Beer/ Wine
SERVING: Lunch/ Dinner (Sundays dinner only)
PRICE RANGE: $$
Another great restaurant from the Amici folks that has the great authentic Italian ambience and cuisine we all expect. The menu is filled with classics such as thin

crust pizzas, many pastas, artichoke and hearts of palm salad, and the traditional osso buco.

ANIMAL RESTAURANT
435 N Fairfax Ave, Los Angeles, 323-782-9225
www.animalrestaurant.com
CUISINE: American (New)
DRINKS: Beer & Wine Only
SERVING: Dinner, Brunch on Sat & Sun
PRICE RANGE: $$$
NEIGHBORHOOD: Beverly Grove
Trendy eatery situated in a rather severe long narrow room with nothing on the walls and plain wooden

tables filling the apace. (I'm thankful to a reader named Jim Bryant from Laguna Beach who told me about this place.) A harsh white light radiates from above, but at night they turn this off and it's more subdued and less Spartan. A little wine bar is at the back of the space. They serve up excellent meat delicacies with interesting twists. I am not a fan of the space—it looks like it was "designed" by, well, no one. What I DO like, however, is the slightly daring food. Favorites: Boner Burger (bone marrow mixed with ground chuck/short rib—this thing is wonderfully, dangerously rich) and Braised rabbit legs. Basically, small plates meant to share.

CLEMENTINE
1751 Ensley Ave, Los Angeles, 310-552-1080
www.clementineonline.com
CUISINE: Bakery, Cafe
DRINKS: No Booze
SERVING: Breakfast, Lunch
PRICE RANGE: S$
NEIGHBORHOOD: Westwood
Chef Annie Miller owns this neighborhood bakery-café that offers a nice menu of soups, salads, sandwiches and entrees. Great breakfast menu and selection of pre-made entrees to go. There's also a nice selection of pastries and gift baskets.

CULINA
300 S Doheny Dr, Los Angeles, 310-860-4000
www.culinarestaurant.com
CUISINE: Italian
DRINKS: Full Bar
SERVING: Breakfast, Lunch, Dinner
PRICE RANGE: $$$
NEIGHBORHOOD: Beverly Grove
Located in the Four Seasons Hotel, this Italian restaurant adds a modern twist to the classic dishes and has been lauded for their efforts. A great choice for lunch as its comfortable and there's free valet parking (a plus in L.A.). The menu features a variety of crudos, sandwiches, handmade pastas and pizzas. Menu favorites include: Ricciola made with Hawaiian yellow tail with persimmon, pear and chive and Salmon with Venetian black rice, basil, shallots and tomatoes. Delicious foccacia is served while you're ordering. Great spot for Sunday brunch.

CUT
9500 Wilshire Blvd., Beverly Hills: 310-276-8500
www.wolfgangpuck.com
CUISINE: Steakhouse
DRINKS: Full Bar
SERVING: Dinner
PRICE RANGE: S$$$

CUT restaurant, the newest addition to the Beverly Wilshire Four Seasons, has created a sense of chic within the hotel's former classically modeled dining room. Designed by architect Richard Meier, CUT is large, lustrous, and smooth, with oak floors, black-and-white trimmings, and curling vines budding alongside the walls of the two-level fortress. The menu offers USDA Prime, Kobe beef, and true Japanese 100% Wagyu beef from Kagoshima, all of which are complemented by an assortment of tangy sauces, an array of vegetables, and a smart wine list. The elegance of CUT is sure to impress.

E. BALDI
375 N Canon Dr, Beverly Hills, 310-248-2633
www.ebaldi.com
CUISINE: Italian
DRINKS: Full Bar
SERVING: Lunch & Dinner; closed Sun & Mon
PRICE RANGE: $$$
NEIGHBORHOOD: Beverly Hills

Upscale power dining spot serving exceptional Italian entrees and desserts. Fun and exciting. Table 1, which is right next to the entrance and the biggest in the house, is reserved for entertainment industry heavyweights. The tables are so closely packed here that you'll be able to eavesdrop on any conversation at tables next to you. My Favorites: Mixed seafood grill; Lasagna (not on the menu, but you can ask for it); Seared tuna and Margherita Pizza. Wonderful bread served with tomatoes and olive oil. Reservations recommended.

THE GRILL ON THE ALLEY
9560 Dayton Way, Beverly Hills, 310-276-0615
www.thegrill.com
CUISINE: Seafood, Steakhouse
DRINKS: Full Bar
SERVING: Lunch, Dinner
PRICE RANGE: $$$
NEIGHBORHOOD: Beverly Hills
Opened as a tribute to the great American grills of yesterday, the menu is classic American serving prime steaks, seafood, and traditional dishes. Menu favorites include: Chicken Hash and Meatloaf with mashed potatoes. A popular power lunch destination for agents, studio heads and celebrities. Hard to get a table at lunch. Best bet is to arrive early and nab a seat at the bar. That's what I do. It's fun talking to the bartenders. (They've seen it all, let me tell you.)

HINOKI & THE BIRD
10 W Century Dr, Los Angeles, 310-552-1200
www.hinokiandthebird.com
CUISINE: American (New) / Asian bistro
DRINKS: Full Bar
SERVING: Lunch & Dinner
PRICE RANGE: $$$

NEIGHBORHOOD: Century City
Romantic dining spot with an inspired menu and creative cocktails is frequented by staff at the nearby CAA, the biggest talent agency in town. The Fox lot is close by as well, so lots of people rush over here for lunch. Hard to get a table between noon and 2. The bar scene here get crowded as well, filling the moment everybody leaves work at 5, so it's a great place to hang out to meet people in the entertainment industry. The beautifully landscaped back patio is a big plus. My Favorites: Buttered Lobster ramen is a specialty here; Salmon with brown rice; Roasted Duck. Nice upscale dining experience.

HOTVILLE CHICKEN
4070 Marlton Ave, Los Angeles, 323-792-4835
www.hotvillechicken.com
CUISINE: Fried Chicken Nashville-style

DRINKS: No Booze
SERVING: Lunch & Dinner (except Monday, when it's closed)
PRICE RANGE: $$
NEIGHBORHOOD: Baldwin Hills / Crenshaw
Known for Nashville-style hot chicken, this is just one of the many chicken spots in this neighborhood. But this one is run by a member of the Prince family that originated Hot Chicken in Nashville in the 1930s. Favorites: Fried Fish and Mac & Cheese.

IL CIELO
9018 Burton Way, Beverly Hills: 310-276-9990
www.ilcielo.com
CUISINE: Italian
DRINKS: Full Bar
SERVING: Lunch/ Dinner
PRICE RANGE: $$$

In this confection of a restaurant, Il Cielo presents a wondrously elegant and stunningly romantic setting that is sure to bewitch even the most cosmopolitan of patrons. Owner and Executive Chef Pasquale Vericella has meticulously created a destination restaurant where guests can bask in the charms of Il Cielo's visual beauty and revel in its exquisite Northern Italian cuisine. Nestled in a residential area of fabled Beverly Hills a couple miles east of Rodeo Drive, Il Cielo beguiles guests with a captivating romantic beauty created by its casually elegant décor, twinkling lights, and lush foliage.

KISMET ROTISSERIE
4666 Hollywood Blvd, Los Angeles, 323-400-3700
www.kismet.family/
CUISINE: Chicken-rotisserie / Mediterranean
DRINKS: No Booze
SERVING: Lunch & Dinner
PRICE RANGE: $$

NEIGHBORHOOD: East Hollywood
Small eatery that's mainly a grab a quick lunch type of place, but the fact that the chicken here is so good doesn't make that a casual statement. (Most of the seating is outside.) Favorite dish: Rotisserie chicken, pure and simple. Indoor & outdoor seating.

LA SCALA
434 N Canon Dr., Beverly Hills: 310-275-0579
www.lascalabeverlyhills.com
CUISINE: Italian
DRINKS: Full Bar
SERVING: Lunch/ Dinner
PRICE RANGE: $$$
Since opening in 1956, La Scala has been popular with the locals and entertainment industry with its comfortable red booths and drawings of Hollywood figures lining the walls. Draws tops agent from UTA, Gersh and Paradigm, whose offices are within walking distance. No reservations, and they make you wait if you have a guest running late, which to bigwigs in Hollywood is insufferable. Traditional Italian fare is offered, as well as an exceptional wine list supplied by Owner Jean Leon's personal vineyard, Chateau Leon, in Spain. The restaurant is revered for its Chopped Salad. (Not on the menu is the semi-secret Bolognese alternative, but you can order it.) Other menu highlights include the Steamed Mussels served in a broth of garlic, white wine and tomato sauce, and the Tiramisu served with fresh whipped cream and berries. The quality of ingredients has never faltered in the restaurant's long history, and it continues to set the bar for fine Italian fare.

MARIPOSA
9700 Wilshire Blvd, Beverly Hills, 310-975-4350
www.neimanmarcus.com
CUISINE: American
DRINKS: Full Bar
SERVING: Lunch
PRICE RANGE: S$$
NEIGHBORHOOD: Beverly Hills
A perfect respite from shopping, this refined eatery offers a relaxing atmosphere for a cocktail or a quick lunch. If you're an early shopper, try brunch. Menu favorites include: Lobster Club and Honey-Roasted Mirin Glazed Salmon. This place may seem a little outdated with the model going from table to table but the food is good.

MIZLALA
5400 West Adams Blvd, Los Angeles, 323-433-7137
No web site
CUISINE: Mediterranean / Falafels
DRINKS: Beer & Wine Only
SERVING: Lunch & Dinner; Closed Mondays
PRICE RANGE: $
NEIGHBORHOOD: West Adams (also a location in Sherman Oaks)
Mediterranean restaurant with a creative though short menu featuring Moroccan fried chicken and other Middle Eastern dishes. This is one of the best examples of Middle Eastern food to be found in L.A. It's also one of the most bare-bones places I mention

in this book—the food is just so very good. There's just basically a counter inside where you order. The outside patio is nice—a sprinkling of tables among a few scrubby trees.

MR. CHOW
344 N Camden Dr., Beverly Hills: 310-278-9911
www.mrchow.com
CUISINE: Chinese
DRINKS: Full Bar
SERVING: Lunch/ Dinner
PRICE RANGE: $$$$

Its sleek, artsy aesthetic, chic clientele, and inventive twists on traditional Chinese cuisine have distinguished Mr. Chow as a Beverly Hills hot spot since 1974. Avid art collector, restaurateur, and self-proclaimed Renaissance man, Michael Chow has a sixth sense for detecting the direction of cultural zeitgeists, producing numerous restaurants that instantly become magnets for all who are harbingers of cool. (As long as you have Cash to go with your Cool.) Mr. Chow's Beverly Hills location is no exception, attracting celebrities, artists and those not so famous who want to see them. With its stylish black and white décor, original Andy Warhols, and decadent dishes, even the most proletariat of diners can treat themselves to a night of Hollywood glamour and posh pampering at Mr. Chow for some ridiculously expensive Chinese food.

N/NAKA
3455 S. Overland Ave., Culver City: 310-836-6252

www.n-naka.com
CUISINE: Japanese
DRINKS: Beer & wine
SERVING: Dinner nightly from 6
PRICE RANGE: $$$$
Focuses on *kaiseki*, or as they call it here, "Modern Kaiseki." (Runs about $150 per person.) You get about a dozen little tidbits in a multi-course meal. Also offers a vegetarian version of this multicourse meal. They take things so seriously here, however, that I usually don't have "fun."

THE PALM
267 N Canon Dr., Los Angeles, 310-550-8811
www.thepalm.com
CUISINE: Steakhouse
DRINKS: Full Bar
SERVING: Lunch & Dinner; Dinner only Sat & Sun
PRICE RANGE: $$$
NEIGHBORHOOD: Downtown
L.A.'s outpost of the classic New York chain known as the "granddaddy of steakhouses." Attracts talent agents from CAA, UTA and WME. Classy dining experience with the biggest lobsters west of the Mississippi. Filets are infamous and the Lobster Mac 'n Cheese is a must. (The Palm also has a location in Downtown.)

PIZZANA
11712 San Vicente Blvd, Los Angeles, 310-481-7108
www.pizzana.com
CUISINE: Pizza / Italian
DRINKS: Beer & Wine Only
SERVING: Lunch & Dinner
PRICE RANGE: $$
NEIGHBORHOOD: Brentwood
Modern eatery featuring thin-crust pizza and Italian fare. Maybe it's the "imported Italian flour" that makes the crust so delicious. I'm not sure, but whatever it is, it works. With over a dozen solid pizza selections, you'll find something you'll love. Antipasti selections as well. Gluten free and vegan options are available. They cook the veggies over wood, so they have a nice flavor. A few tables outside. Fair selection of wines.

POLO LOUNGE
9641 Sunset Blvd., Beverly Hills: 310-276-2251
www.dorchestercollection.com
CUISINE: American
DRINKS: Full Bar
SERVING: Breakfast/ Lunch/ Dinner
PRICE RANGE: $$$$

Located in the Beverly Hills Hotel, Polo Lounge has been a favorite for lunching socialites and Hollywood locals for generations. The lush dining room features massive booths surrounded by dark green and cream-striped walls, while the delightful patio is surrounded by flowering vines and pink archways. Serving a traditional yet elegant cuisine, the menu features favorites like honey-pepper cured smoked salmon and steak tartare. Lots of power lunching ladies in the film business order the McCarthy Salad, made famous here when it went on the menu in 1948 at the behest of lawyer Neil McCarthy. He had the kitchen create a salad with his own mix of ingredients: iceberg, romaine, beets, cheddar, smoked bacon, hard-boiled eggs, grilled chicken, tomatoes and balsamic vinegar. People at the Regent **Beverly Wilshire** say this iconic salad was actually invented there. And while it's not on the menu, you can still order it. (It'll make you look like an insider.)

SOUTH BEVERLY GRILL
122 S Beverly Dr, Beverly Hills, 310-550-0242
www.southbeverlygrill.com
CUISINE: American (New) / Seafood
DRINKS: Full Bar

SERVING: Lunch & Dinner
PRICE RANGE: $$$
NEIGHBORHOOD: Beverly Hills
Warm, cozy upscale eatery. If you're seeking to have a business lunch in a nice place that won't cost you the shirt on your back, this is the place to go. The booths and warm dark ambience give it a "private" feel. It also boasts the most pleasant servers in all of L.A., or so it seems to me. Offers a creative healthy menu. My Favorites: Grilled chicken salad and Coconut shrimp sushi roll.

SUGARFISH BEVERLY HILLS
212 N Canon Dr, Beverly Hills, 310-276-6900
www.sugarfishsushi.com
CUISINE: Sushi / Japanese
DRINKS: Beer & Wine
SERVING: Lunch & Dinner
PRICE RANGE: $$$
NEIGHBORHOOD: Beverly Hills
Very popular spot (they have several locations here in L.A., so check the web site to see which one is closest to you) and you can expect a wait for your table at peak times because they don't take reservations. Great selection of sushi. My Favorites: Nozawa omakase; Blue crab hand roll; Scallop nigiri. Tip: sit at the bar if you want fast service.

SUSHI SASABUNE
9162 W Olympic Blvd, Beverly Hills, 310-859-3878
11917 Wilshire Blvd, Los Angeles, 310-478-3596
101 N Brand Blvd, Glendale, 818-696-1124
WEB SITE down at press time

CUISINE: Sushi / Japanese / American (New)
DRINKS: Beer & Wine
SERVING: Lunch & Dinner, Dinner only on Sat; closed Sun
PRICE RANGE: $$$$
NEIGHBORHOOD: Beverly Hills / Brentwood / Glendale

Authentic upscale sushi eatery with just about 40 seats to handle the numerous regulars that haunt this place, located in an unimpressive strip mall. Impressive menu, mostly traditional nigiri and sashimis. Everything here is extremely fresh and flavorful. There's an "omakase" lunch special, and it's the best thing to do. Has an outpost in far-away Glendale

SUSHI ZO
9824 National Blvd., Cheviot Hills, nr. Culver City: 424-201-5576
www.sushizo.us
CUISINE: Japanese
DRINKS: Beer & wine only
SERVING: Lunch weekdays; dinner Mon-Sat; closed Sun
PRICE RANGE: $$$$

Keizo Seki, the boss here, doesn't tart up his fish like a lot of other "Americanized" sushi joints. It's plainer than other places, purists would say better. (This guy even makes his own soy sauce.)

SPAGO
176 N Canon Dr., Beverly Hills: 310-385-0880
www.wolfgangpuck.com

CUISINE: American / Asian Fusion
DRINKS: Full Bar
SERVING: Dinner
PRICE RANGE: $$$$

The flagship Wolfgang Puck restaurant offers cuisine that is at the forefront of the Los Angeles culinary scene. Executive Chef Lee Hefter is both inventive and playful, creating masterful combinations of the freshest and finest ingredients. Famous dishes include the Handmade Agnolotti with mascarpone, Chino Farms Roasted Beet Layer Cake, and Prime Côte du Boeuf for Two. The menu changes seasonally to showcase the best of California's produce, and the Chef's eight-course tasting menu is an ideal way to sample the best that Hefter has to offer at any one time. The chic restaurant is also known for its celebrity spotting, including Wolfgang Puck himself.

THE STINKING ROSE
55 North La Cienega Blvd., Beverly Hills: 310-652-7673
www.thestinkingrose.com

CUISINE: American / Italian
DRINKS: Full Bar
SERVING: Daily lunch and dinner
PRICE RANGE: $$

If your idea of a great meal is garlic, garlic, and more garlic, head to Restaurant Row on La Cienega and visit The Stinking Rose. Executive Chef and owner Andrea Froncillo has created a garlic lover's paradise, featuring great food in a wildly fun, garlic-themed atmosphere. Fantastic for large parties, the restaurant boasts a varied menu with specialties including roasted crab, prime rib, pastas, and giant tureens of steamed clams, all bathed in garlic. Don't forget to visit "Dracula's Grotto," one of many ornately decorated rooms, and to try Gilroy's Famous Garlic Ice Cream.

TOSCANOVA
10250 Santa Monica Blvd, Los Angeles, 310-551-0499
https://toscanova.com/
CUISINE: Italian
DRINKS: Full Bar
SERVING: Lunch, Dinner
PRICE RANGE: $$$
NEIGHBORHOOD: Century City

This is a popular spot for a power lunch or a first date and great for people watching on the patio. The food is very good here with a menu of classic Italian dishes. Menu favorites include: Prosciutto pizza and Tagliatelle Alla Bolognese.
The bartenders take joy in serving special cocktails and the homemade desserts are worth a try.

Chapter 2
WEST HOLLYWOOD & HOLLYWOOD

DID YOU FIND AN INTERESTING PLACE?
If you discover a place you think I should check out on my next visit, drop me a line, will you? I'll mention your name if I end up listing it.
andrewdelaplaine@mac.com

AUBURN
6703 Melrose Ave, Los Angeles, 323-486-6703
www.auburnla.com
CUISINE: American (New)
DRINKS: Full Bar

SERVING: Dinner, Lunch & Dinner on Sat & Sun; Closed Mon & Tues
PRICE RANGE: $$$$
NEIGHBORHOOD: Hollywood
Minimalist upscale eatery with a menu of a dozen individual plates in the main dining room. Or you can order *à la carte* in the bar, which I actually prefer. Favorites: Deep fried Pig Ears and Chopped Lamb tartare. A true dining experience. Impressive wine list. Reservations recommended.

BIRDS
5925 Franklin Ave., Los Angeles: 323-465-0175
www.birdshollywood.com
CUISINE: American
DRINKS: Full Bar
SERVING: Lunch/ Dinner
PRICE RANGE: $$
Great place for casual eating and drinking. The sauces they have for the rotisserie chicken (especially the artichoke sauce) is delicious. Very trendy. Its next to the Upright Citizens Brigade Theatre for live comedy and performances.

BOA STEAKHOUSE
9200 Sunset Blvd., West Hollywood: 310-278-2050
www.boasteak.com
CUISINE: Steakhouse
DRINKS: Full Bar
SERVING: Lunch/ Dinner
PRICE RANGE: $$$$
Coming from Beverly Hills into WEHO, BOA is one of the first places to stop for happy hour down the sunset strip. It is great spot for film biz people. The steak, delicious. It can definitely get very crowded.

CECCONI'S
8764 Melrose Ave, West Hollywood, 310-432-2000
www.cecconiswesthollywood.com
CUISINE: Italian / Steakhouse
DRINKS: Full Bar
SERVING: Lunch, Dinner
PRICE RANGE: $$$

NEIGHBORHOOD: West Hollywood
This is a favorite brunch spot and great for people watching. Here you'll find an affordable menu of classic Italian cuisine as well as cicchetti (Italian tapas). Menu favorites include: Gnocci pasta, meatballs, and pizza. There are three areas: the main dining room, the terrace (where you'll feel like you're in Europe) and the bar. Nice wine list. Free valet parking, a real surprise in this town.

CHATEAU MARMONT
8221 Sunset Blvd., West Hollywood: 323-656-1010
www.chateaumarmont.com
CUISINE: American / Burgers
DRINKS: Full Bar
SERVING: Dinner/ Late Night
PRICE RANGE: $$$
Modeled after an infamous royal residence in France's Loire Valley, this is definitely the place to see movie industry types. Outside you can see the paparazzi

waiting for celebrities. No pictures are allowed in the restaurant area.

CHI SPACCA
6610 Melrose Ave, Los Angeles, 323-297-1133
www.chispacca.com
CUISINE: Italian
DRINKS: Beer & Wine
SERVING: Dinner
PRICE RANGE: $$$$
NEIGHBORHOOD: Hancock Park
Small Italian grill with meat-focused menu. They have an open kitchen so you can check out all the action. My Favorites: Focaccia di recco and Beef & Bone marrow pie with a flaky crust. A meat eaters' paradise, with some of their cured meats having been aged for as long as 2 years. Creative desserts like cocoa nib caramel tart.

CLEMENTINE
1751 Ensley Ave, Los Angeles, 310-552-1080
www.clementineonline.com
CUISINE: Bakery / Cafe
DRINKS: No Booze
SERVING: Breakfast, Lunch
PRICE RANGE: $$
NEIGHBORHOOD: Westwood
Chef Annie Miller owns this neighborhood bakery-café that offers a nice menu of soups, salads, sandwiches and entrees. Great breakfast menu and selection of pre-made entrees to go. There's also a nice selection of pastries and gift baskets.

CONNIE AND TED'S
8171 Santa Monica Blvd, West Hollywood, 323-848-2722
www.connieandteds.com
CUISINE: Seafood / American (Traditional)
DRINKS: Full Bar
SERVING: Lunch & Dinner, Dinner only on Mon. & Tues.
PRICE RANGE: $$$
NEIGHBORHOOD: West Hollywood
West Hollywood hot spot with a seafood focused menu. My Favorites: Lobster rolls; New England Boiled Dinner (a little bit of everything for those who can't decide). Creative cocktails and desserts. Dine on the patio for a quieter meal. Happy hour.

CRAIG'S
8826 Melrose Ave., West Hollywood: 310-276-1900
www.craigs.la
CUISINE: American

DRINKS: Full Bar
SERVING: Dinner (Lunch to go)
PRICE RANGE: $$$
Located near the Troubadour, this place has great service and delicious food. George Clooney and Grant Heslov held their 2013 Oscar party here for Ben Affleck and "Argo." Very popular place among those in the Industry.

CULINA
300 S Doheny Dr, Los Angeles, 310-860-4000
www.culinarestaurant.com
CUISINE: Italian
DRINKS: Full Bar
SERVING: Breakfast, Lunch, Dinner
PRICE RANGE: S$$
NEIGHBORHOOD: Beverly Grove
Located in the Four Seasons Hotel, this Italian restaurant adds a modern twist to the classic dishes and has been lauded for their efforts. A great choice for lunch as its comfortable and there's free valet parking (a plus in L.A.). The menu features a variety of crudos, sandwiches, handmade pastas and pizzas. Menu favorites include: Ricciola made with Hawaiian yellow tail with persimmon, pear and chive and Salmon with Venetian black rice, basil, shallots and tomatoes. Delicious foccacia is served while you're ordering. Great spot for Sunday brunch.

DAN TANA'S RESTAURANT
9071 Santa Monica Blvd., West Hollywood: 310-275-9444
www.dantanasrestaurant.com

CUISINE: Italian
DRINKS: Full Bar
SERVING: Dinner
PRICE RANGE: $$$
More than a great restaurant, Dan Tana's is the ultimate Hollywood hangout. Boasting a superlative menu and a client list that reads like a Who's Who of Hollywood, Tana's is filled every night with customers who return again and again.

EVELEIGH
8752 W Sunset Blvd., West Hollywood: 424-239-1630
www.theeveleigh.com
CUISINE: American
DRINKS: Full Bar
SERVING: Dinner
PRICE RANGE: $$$
In WeHo, Seasonal menu and large patio. Very nice.

DESTROYER
3578 Hayden Ave, Culver City, 310-360-3860
www.destroyer.la
CUISINE: American (New)
DRINKS: No Booze
SERVING: Breakfast & Lunch; Closed Sat. & Sun.
PRICE RANGE: $$
NEIGHBORHOOD: Culver City / Hayden Tract
Minimalist eatery offering a menu of tiny dishes (changes daily). My Favorites: Raw Oatmeal and Chicken confit.

FIG & OLIVE
8490 Melrose Pl, West Hollywood, 310-360-9100
www.figandolive.com
CUISINE: Mediterranean / French / Vegetarian
DRINKS: Full Bar
SERVING: Lunch & Dinner
PRICE RANGE: $$$
NEIGHBORHOOD: Beverly Grove
L.A. location of the New York-based chain with a simple menu of fresh Mediterranean cuisine served in a beautiful atmosphere. Staff is particularly attentive. Another plus is its closeness to great shopping. My Favorites: Eggplant tapenade and Truffle Risotto. Nice date night spot. Creative cocktails.

THE HART & THE HUNTER
Palihotel
7950 Melrose Ave, Los Angeles, 323-424-3055
www.thehartandthehunter.com
CUISINE: American (New)

DRINKS: Beer & Wine
SERVING: Breakfast, Lunch & Dinner
PRICE RANGE: $$
NEIGHBORHOOD: Beverly Grove
Quirky eatery offering Southern-inspired fare like crispy chicken skin with hot-pepper vinegar, sort of their imitation of a potato chip. Really a fun place to be. The delicious smoked trout is served in a jar, along with pickles, egg and avocado. My Favorites: Shrimp 'n Grits brunch and Coconut-Almond French Toast with Blueberries & Mascarpone. This place makes breakfast the most important meal of the day. Busy & loud, but lots of energy and fun.

HERE'S LOOKING AT YOU
3901 W 6th St, Los Angeles, 213-568-3573
www.hereslookingatyoula.com
CUISINE: American (New)
DRINKS: Full Bar
SERVING: Dinner; closed Tues.
PRICE RANGE: $$$
NEIGHBORHOOD: Koreatown/Wilshire Center
Lively eatery with a real neighborhood atmosphere offers international inspired American fare. Robust cocktail program. My Favorites: Frogs legs served with salsa negra scallions; Steak tartare; Pork Belly is also excellent. Creative cocktails like the Ice Queen (similar to a Pina Colada but without the pineapple).

HOLLYWOOD FARMERS' MARKET
1600 Ivar Ave, Los Angeles, 323-463-3171
www.seela.org
CUISINE: Farmers Market

DRINKS: Full Bar
SERVING: Sundays only 8 a.m. – 1 p.m.
PRICE RANGE: $$
NEIGHBORHOOD: Hollywood
Wonderful farmers' market with a variety of organic produce, foods, fresh oysters, juices, jams, flowers, nuts and local farm harvest. The earlier you go, the more chefs you'll see doing their daily shopping to reinforce that "farm-to-table" mentality that's taken over American restaurants. Food stands with a variety of foods from BBQ to Mexican.

IL PICCOLINO
350 N. Robertson Blvd., West Hollywood, 310-659-2220
www.ilpiccolinorestaurant.com
CUISINE: Italian
DRINKS: Beer and wine
SERVING: Mon – Sat lunch and dinner, Sun closed
PRICE RANGE: $$$
NEIGHBORHOOD: West Hollywood
Famed producer Jerry Weintraub was a regular here, always sitting at the same table. This is a tiny little place, so it's a good idea to book ahead. Very charming family-run place with an emphasis on high quality ingredients. Pastas are divine. The balsamic vinegar here is aged 10 years.

THE IVY
113 N Robertson Blvd., West Hollywood: 310-274-8303
www.theivyrestaurants.com
CUISINE: American
DRINKS: Full Bar
SERVING: Lunch/ Dinner
PRICE RANGE: $$$

The Ivy is a Los Angeles mainstay and is frequented by celebrities. As for the menu, think comfort food, like fried chicken, Cajun prime rib and fish and fresh corn chowder. Request a seat on the famed patio for the best people watching.

KALI
5722 Melrose Ave, Los Angeles, 323-871-4160
www.kalirestaurant.com
CUISINE: American (New)
DRINKS: Full Bar
SERVING: Lunch & Dinner, Dinner only on Sat & Sun
PRICE RANGE: $$$
NEIGHBORHOOD: Larchmont

Unprepossessing exterior masks a chic eatery boasting a Michelin-starred chef offering a menu of contemporary California cuisine. The blond-wood tables and chairs give the place a sleek and casual look, but it's serious underneath it all. The bread they put in front of you is so darned delicious that you'll tend to eat too much of it. DON'T! Save room for the main course. Favorites: Winter mushroom risotto; Sea Urchin Pasta; and Dry Aged Squab. Chef's Menu with wine pairing and seasonal tasting menu. Eclectic wine list.

KATSUYA
6300 Hollywood Blvd., Hollywood: 323-515-8782
www.sbe.com/katsuya
CUISINE: Japanese / Asian Fusion
DRINKS: Full Bar
SERVING: Mon – Fri lunch, Dinner daily
PRICE RANGE: $$$
Trendy spot for film people.

LAUREL HARDWARE
7984 Santa Monica Blvd., West Hollywood: 323-656-6070
www.laurelhardware.com
CUISINE: American
DRINKS: Full bar
SERVING: Daily lunch and dinner
PRICE RANGE: $$$$
Some of the small plates are a little pricey, like cod fritters and pork ribs, but they're damned good. The positive vibe and good-looking crowd help things

along. The cauliflower salad is super. The lamb neck (I know how bad that sounds) is really tasty. Sit under the olive trees outback if the weather's good.

M CAFÉ DE CHAYA
7119 Melrose Ave, Hollywood: 323-525-0588
www.mcafedechaya.com
CUISINE: Japanese / Vegan
DRINKS: No booze, including beer. How can a self-respecting Japanese restaurant not serve beer?
SERVING: Breakfast/ Lunch/ Dinner
PRICE RANGE: $$

One of the hottest new places in Hollywood. If you've been infected with Organica or Macrobiotica, head here now. It's often impossibly crowded and parking's a nightmare. They've got lots of premade things that are handy if you're short on time, otherwise it's better to order fresh, considering how far you'll be set back. Most mains hover around the $10-15 range.

MADEO
8897 Beverly Blvd., Los Angeles, 310-859-4903
www.madeoristorante.com
CUISINE: Italian / American
DRINKS: Full bar
SERVING: Dinner
PRICE RANGE: $$$$
NEIGHBORHOOD: West Hollywood
Attracts celebs like Johnny Depp, Steve Bing and Vanessa Getty. They come for the special branzino they make here as well as the delicately crafted pasta dishes, especially the gnocchi.

MUSSO & FRANK
6667 Hollywood Blvd., Los Angeles, 323-467-7788
www.mussoandfrank.com
CUISINE: Seafood / Steakhouse / American
DRINKS: Full bar
SERVING: Tues – Sat lunch and dinner, Sun – Mon closed
PRICE RANGE: $$$
NEIGHBORHOOD: Hollywood
This place goes way back. Douglas Fairbanks used to eat here. And William Faulkner, before he won the Nobel Prize for Literature in 1949, when he was an unsuccessful hack screenwriter for MGM, used to drink here with one of his pals, director Howard Hawks. The food's still great, almost because it's so unsurprising.

OLIVETTA
9010 Melrose Ave, West Hollywood, 310-307-3932
www.olivetta.la

CUISINE: Italian with flourishes
DRINKS: Full Bar
SERVING: Dinner from 5 nightly
PRICE RANGE: $$
NEIGHBORHOOD: West Hollywood
Fine dining European-style eatery offers an elegant dining experience—in 4 rooms each of which offers a completely different ambience. The main room, however, is the most lush and luxurious. The swooping drapery gives you the feel you're dining in some tarted-up Arabian tent in the desert. Favorites: Spanish style octopus and Yellowtail tartare. Curated cocktails and impressive wine list.

PETIT TROIS
718 Highland Ave., Hollywood: 323-468-8916
http://petittrois.com/
CUISINE: French
DRINKS: Full Bar
SERVING: Lunch / Dinner

PRICE RANGE: $$$
This spot used to be a dumpy Thai eatery in a tacky strip mall till it was beautifully transformed into a charming bistro atmosphere with black & white tiled floors, mirrored wall, marble bar, copper pots hanging in the cramped open kitchen. Only about 20 seats, all stools. Picks: chicken leg confit cooked first in duck fat & then cooked with brioche butter; *sole meuniere* expertly rendered; excellent steak tartare; some of the best bread in L.A., all made by a woman working out of her home—definitely the best French baguette in L.A; fine Boursin cheese omelette (light and fluffy in the French manner, not like the thick slab of eggs you get in most American places); hand-cut fries are cooked in beef fat, very crispy; parsley butter escargots; onion soup has a thick top of Gruyere and Emmenthal cheese that will keep you coming back. Try the Mauresque cocktail (pastis & pear brandy). One of my absolute favorite spots in L.A.

PINK'S HOT DOGS
709 N. La Brea Avenue, West Hollywood: 323-931-4223
www.pinkshollywood.com
CUISINE: American / Hot dogs
DRINKS: Full Bar
SERVING: Lunch/ Dinner/ Late Night
PRICE RANGE: $
Serving the most famous hot dogs in Los Angeles since 1939, their chili dog will set you back just $4. Pink's is the ultimate Mom and Pop hot dog stand. It's a Hollywood love story, starting with Paul & Betty Pink selling hot dogs from a cart on a neighborhood

street corner at La Brea & Melrose in 1939. Then the city fell in love with the tasty chili dogs and friendly service, and 73 years later, Pink's has become a Hollywood landmark and internationally famous, now operated by Paul & Betty's family -- Richard, Gloria, and Beverly. The Pink family has even expanded to ten locations including Southern California, Las Vegas, and Ohio.

SALT'S CURE
1155 N Highland Ave, Los Angeles, 323-465-7258
https://saltscure.com/
CUISINE: American (New) / Vegetarian / Seafood
DRINKS: Full Bar
SERVING: Lunch & Dinner
PRICE RANGE: $$
NEIGHBORHOOD: Hollywood
Small meat-centric eatery serving rustic American seasonal fare that they brag was all raised in

California. They buy all the animals they serve here whole and butcher them in-house. Similarly, they make their own bacon and even the ketchup in-house. My Favorites: Start with the wood baked sourdough bread; Chicken liver mousse; Chili braised pork shoulder; Oatmeal Griddle Cakes and Ol' Salty's Bacon Cheeseburger. Casual atmosphere with outside patio. Don't leave without trying one of their pecan donut holes with a coffee glaze.

SOPRANO
6263 Hollywood Blvd (at Vine), Los Angeles, 323-879-4100
www.sopranola.com
CUISINE: Italian
DRINKS: Full Bar

SERVING: Dinner; Closed Mondays
PRICE RANGE: $$
NEIGHBORHOOD: Hollywood
Located next door to the famed historic Pantages Theater, this makes a perfect pre-theater dining choice. Also for those tourists strolling down the Hollywood Walk of Fame. From the high-ceilinged dining room, you can look out on the famous corner of Hollywood & Vine. Favorites: Meatballs with pork & beef; Rigatoni Bolognese (a must-try). Save room for their incredible Tiramisu.

SPOON BY H
7158 Beverly Blvd, Los Angeles, 323-930-0789
www.spoonbyh.com
CUISINE: Korean
DRINKS: No Booze
SERVING: Lunch & Dinner; closed Sunday
PRICE RANGE: S
NEIGHBORHOOD: Fairfax
Casual counter-serve café featuring homestyle Korean fare. Favorites: Shaved Snow (in Coffee,

chocolate, Caramel flavors); Homemade Waffles and Boba Tea Sandwich. Fresh juices, coffees, teas and smoothies.

SUSHI PARK
8539 Sunset Blvd., West Hollywood: 310-652-0523
NO WEBSITE (along with a lot of other No-no's)
CUISINE: Sushi
DRINKS: Beer and wine
SERVING: Mon – Fri lunch and dinner, Sat dinner only, Sun closed
PRICE RANGE: $$$$
This may be a high-end sushi bar, but it's also one of the most invisible ones in all of LA. It's located on the second floor of a drab strip mall, not something that generates enthusiasm. But it's so authentic it draws people like Charlize Theron. You'll notice a sign when you go in that says, "No California rolls!"

TROIS MEC
716 N Highland Ave, Los Angeles, 323-484-8588
www.troismec.com
CUISINE: French
DRINKS: Full Bar
SERVING: Dinner; Closed Sun & Mon
PRICE RANGE: $$$$
NEIGHBORHOOD: Hollywood
Unique eatery set in a former pizza joint in a nondescript strip mall, this place has a constantly changing menu with a fixed tasting menu. No reservations – you purchase "tickets" like going to the theater, prepaying in advance. Email to info@troismec.com for reservations up to 3 weeks in advance. Impressive wine list.

VIALE DEI ROMANI
627 N La Peer Dr, West Hollywood, 310-691-1600
www.vialedeiromani.com

CUISINE: Italian
DRINKS: Full Bar
SERVING: Breakfast, Lunch, & Dinner
PRICE RANGE: $$$
NEIGHBORHOOD: West Hollywood
Located in the Kimpton **La Peer Hotel**, this upscale Italian eatery features dishes from seafood to pizza. There's a nice little Courtyard Bar where you can get drinks by the pool. Menu picks: Mackerel with burnt lemon and Tagliatelle with rabbit, sweetbreads, mushrooms & sage.

Chapter 3
Downtown

Koreatown – Chinatown – Wilshire – Little Tokyo – La Brea – East Hollywood

DID YOU FIND AN INTERESTING PLACE?
If you discover a place you think I should check out on my next visit, drop me a line, will you? I'll mention your name if I end up listing it.
andrewdelaplaine@mac.com

ALL DAY BABY
3200 W Sunset Blvd, Los Angeles, 323-741-0082
www.alldaybabyla.com

CUISINE: American (New)
DRINKS: Full Bar
SERVING: Breakfast & Lunch
PRICE RANGE: $$
NEIGHBORHOOD: Silver Lake
The name is confusing as they are not really open all day, they close at 3 p.m. clean lines, sleek design. Popular eatery among locals serving fancied-up American diner fare. Favorites: Pork loin baguette and Whitefish plate. Brunch destination with variations of classics like French Toast with pineapple jam and rum whipped butter.

ANA MARIA
Grand Central Market
317 S Broadway, Los Angeles, 213-620-0477
CUISINE: Mexican
DRINKS: No Booze

SERVING: 9 a.m. – 6 p.m.
PRICE RANGE: $
NEIGHBORHOOD: Downtown
Popular eatery, so expect a line at peak times. Typical Mexican street fare like tacos and tortillas. But it's the Gorditas that really inspire me. Succulent pork and fillings that offer a crunchy texture make it all come together. Huge portions.

BÄCO MERCAT
408 S. Main St., Los Angeles: 213-687-8808
www.bacomercat.com
CUISINE: Spanish / Gastropub
DRINKS: Full bar
SERVING: Daily lunch and dinner
PRICE RANGE: $$
NEIGHBORHOOD: Downtown
What is a "bäco," you might ask? Well, it's a sandwich—a flatbread sandwich, if you will—made with beef carnitas and pork belly. The chef here, Josef Centeno (who previously worked at La Côte Basque and Daniel in New York), invented it as a snack for friends. It took off in popularity, and is the focus of his hot eatery in Downtown. These tasty sandwiches also come with other fillings: crispy shrimp, for instance, or oxtail hash, each more delectable and fattening than the next. This item may be fattening as Hell, but it tastes like Heaven. Try their Bäco Pop, a soda they make in house using ginger, juniper and orange.

BAR AMÁ
118 W 4th St, Los Angeles, 213-687-8002

www.bar-ama.com
CUISINE: Tex-Mex
DRINKS: Full Bar
SERVING: Lunch & Dinner
PRICE RANGE: $$$
NEIGHBORHOOD: Downtown
Tex-Mex eatery offering creative menu by Chef Josef Centeno with items like: Fideo and borracho beans with cilantro and pork belly or Puffy tacos stuffed with legua carnitas and crushed avocado. Tasty cocktails. Delicious desserts like the Leche quemada pudding. Warning: the place gets very loud.

BAR RESTAURANT
4326 Sunset Blvd, Los Angeles, 323-347-5557
www.barrestaurant.la
CUISINE: French
DRINKS: Full Bar
SERVING: Dinner
PRICE RANGE: $$

NEIGHBORHOOD: Silver Lake
Neo bistro offering a French (of a sort) dining experience with favorites like Lamb tartare (don't see that very often); a lovely Frisée; Mussels with Dijon & curly fries. The 16-oz dry-aged sirloin strip is quite nice, but that might have a lot to do with the delicious tomato bordelaise that comes with it. Impressive wine list. Indoor & outdoor seating.

BAVEL
500 Mateo St, Los Angeles, 213-232-4966
www.baveldtla.com
CUISINE: Middle-Eastern

DRINKS: Full Bar
SERVING: Dinner
PRICE RANGE: $$$
NEIGHBORHOOD: Arts District, Downtown
From the people who brought you the popular downtown **BESTIA**, this Middle Eastern eatery has been attracting crowds (reservations often needed 2 months in advance). It's got both indoor and outdoor seating, but the dramatic effect of dozens of 10-foot-long plants dangling from the ceiling is quite impressive. Both inside and out, you're surrounded by GREENERY. They aren't trying to distract you with this onslaught of nature, however, because the food stands up to the most rigorous demands of excellence. One wishes they were open for lunch, but alas, they aren't. Favorites: Braised Wagyu Beef Cheek Tagine and Grilled Prawns. Save room for one of their amazing desserts like the Almond Blossom Honey Nougat Glacé. Cocktails are as creative as the menu.

BESTIA
2121 E Seventh Pl., Los Angeles, 213-514-5724
www.bestiala.com
CUISINE: Italian
DRINKS: Full Bar
SERVING: Dinner
PRICE RANGE: S$$
NEIGHBORHOOD: Downtown
Popular eatery offering a great dining experience in a space with an industrial style design down in the Warehouse District. Hand cut pastas are exemplary. My Favorites: Burrata Pizza and Pan-Roasted

Chicken Gizzards. Great pastas. Impressive wine list. Reservations necessary.

BELCAMPO MEAT CO.
Grand Central Market
317 S Broadway, Los Angeles, 213-625-0304
www.belcampo.com
CUISINE: American (New)/Burgers
DRINKS: Beer & Wine
SERVING: Lunch & Dinner
PRICE RANGE: $$
NEIGHBORHOOD: Downtown
Butcher shop and restaurant offering counter seats and take-out menu. A meat-lovers' paradise. But try to force yourself to get the burger. It's made with dry-aged beef slathered with a layer of caramelized onions and a thick slab of cheddar cheese. The soft as air bun soaks up all the juices. Everything from beef,

pork, goat, lamb, quail, rabbit, squab, and chicken. They also offer a variety of deli meats, bacon, sausages, and eggs. Vegetarian options available.

BLUE COW KITCHEN
350 S. Grand Ave., Los Angeles: 213-621-2249
www.bluecowkitchen.com
CUISINE: American
DRINKS: Full bar
SERVING: Mon – Fri lunch and dinner, Sat dinner, Sun closed
PRICE RANGE: $$
NEIGHBORHOOD: Downtown
You've heard of the "fine fast food" to be had from the Mendocino Farms sandwich shops, right? Here they so the same thing, but you get to sit and enjoy it on premise. The sandwiches are very creative: there's a buttermilk fried chicken sandwich that I love, served with mustard pickle slaw and pimento cheese on mini Hawaiian rolls. A few large plates are also offered. They only buy from local farms and support local food artisans when possible. Also features seasonal cocktails and excellent craft beers.

BON TEMPS
712 S Santa Fe Ave, Los Angeles, 213-784-0044
www.bontempsla.com
CUISINE: French (mostly)
DRINKS: Full Bar
SERVING: Lunch & Dinner, Dinner only on Sat & Sun
PRICE RANGE: $$$
NEIGHBORHOOD: Downtown
Modern bistro with a cheerful interior with white-painted ceilings and exposed a/c ductwork serving French classics and seafood dishes (though, to be honest, it's more of an International menu than a French one). An outdoor area is nice when the weather's good. Favorites: Seared Maine Scallops and Creekstone Prime Flat Iron. They have a great Whole Chicken (Jidori Style) which I suggest you try—it's just bursting with flavor—but it's only available 3 nights a week, Fri-Sun. Creative cocktails like the Blackberry Cobbler (gin, sherry, port, lemon, blackberry). Reservations recommended.

BOTTEGA LOUIE
700 S. Grand Ave., Los Angeles: 213-802-1470
www.bottegalouie.com
CUISINE: Italian
DRINKS: Full bar
SERVING: Mon – Fri breakfast, lunch, and dinner, Sat – Sun brunch and dinner
PRICE RANGE: $$$
NEIGHBORHOOD: Downtown
If the high level of noisy conversation doesn't put you off (and I love it), first sidle up to the marble-topped bar here for some creative specialty cocktails. Then grab a table and chow down the poached lobster soup or a pizza from their wood-burning oven. (The white ones are especially tasty.) Big selection of pasta dishes like the homemade Orecchiette with fennel sausage, radicchio, soppressata, caramelized sweet onions & extra virgin olive oil. Main plates include chops and steaks. Side dishes are really good, but pricey. (Don't overlook this place for breakfast. Grab a croissant and a double macchiato.)

CHICHEN ITZA
Mercado La Paloma
3655 S Grand Ave, Los Angeles, 213-741-1075
www.chichenitzarestaurant.com
CUISINE: Mexican
DRINKS: No Booze
SERVING: Breakfast, Lunch & Dinner
PRICE RANGE: $$
NEIGHBORHOOD: Downtown

Looking for Yucatán grub? This is the place, tucked away inside the sprawling Mercado La Paloma food hall just south of Downtown. The place was featured on 'Diners Drive-ins and Dives'. My Favorites: Cochinita pibil dish and Pollo Asado (Boneless chicken legs cooked over mesquite charcoal). Nice selection of tacos, sandwiches and soups.

CHURCH & STATE
1850 Industrial St., Los Angeles: 213-405-1434
www.churchandstatebistro.com
CUISINE: French bistro
DRINKS: Full bar
SERVING: Mon – Fri lunch and dinner, Fri –Sun dinner only
PRICE RANGE: $$$
NEIGHBORHOOD: Downtown
The Beaux-Arts building in which you find this place really helps to make you feel you're in a bistro, as do the red brick and white subway tile walls and mirrors.

The excellent food completes the fantasy. The place is always packed and an air of bustling excitement fills the place, enhanced by the open kitchen where no one stops working. Roasted bone marrow and pork belly over a bed of polenta gets raves. I also like the onion tarte with applewood smoked bacon and caramelized onions. The salumi here comes from small batch supplies and is excellent. They have a prix-fixe menu on Sunday called "Church on Sundays" that's a good bet. Specialty cocktails.

CLARK STREET BREAD & PASTRY
331 Glendale Blvd, Los Angeles, 213-529-4252
www.clarkstreetbakery.com
CUISINE: Bakery / Breakfast / Lunch
DRINKS: No Booze

SERVING: 7:30 a.m. – 4 p.m.
PRICE RANGE: $$
NEIGHBORHOOD: Westlake (between Filipinotown & Echo Park)
Lovely order-at-the-counter type eatery. Mostly bakery items like croissants and breads but a small menu includes sandwiches, quiche, and dessert. Communal seating.

COLE'S
118 E 6th St., Los Angeles: 213-622-4090
www.colesfrenchdip.com
CUISINE: Sandwiches
DRINKS: Full Bar
SERVING: Lunch/ Dinner/ Late Night
PRICE RANGE: $$
Noted for its French dip sandwiches. You've never had a French dip sandwich like this one, I promise you. Next door to **The Varnish**, a great bar where Ryan Gosling was once seen cadging smokes from a customer.

DAIKOKUYA
327 E. 1st St., Los Angeles: 213-626-1680
www.dkramen.com
CUISINE: Japanese
DRINKS: Beer and wine
SERVING: Daily lunch and dinner
PRICE RANGE: $$
NEIGHBORHOOD: Little Tokyo
If you know your Japanese food, Little Tokyo ion general and this place in particular will be heaven on earth for you. Throughout the district you'll find Japanese comfort food served at the lowest possible prices. Ramen and *tsukemen* served in pork broth with soy-marinated hard boiled eggs, bean sprouts and slender egg noodles they make right here. After that, go after the pork *gyoza* dumplings.

DINO'S CHICKEN AND BURGERS
2525 W. Pico Blvd., Los Angeles: 213-380-3554
www.dinoschicken.com
CUISINE: Burgers / Mexican
DRINKS: No
SERVING: Daily Breakfast/Lunch/Dinner
PRICE RANGE: $
This family-run shop cranks out incredible chicken, prepared with a Greek marinade, and served with a tortilla and coleslaw. "It's one extremely juicy situation," Patterson says. "You're licking your fingers. Don't bother with the napkin." He also likes the family atmosphere, with father and daughters working the counter side by side.

DTLA CHEESE
Grand Central Market
317 S Broadway, Ste 45, Los Angeles, 213-290-3060
www.dtlacheese.com
CUISINE: Cheese shop
DRINKS: No Booze
SERVING: 10 a.m. – 6 p.m. Mon – Wed, 10 a.m. – 8 p.m. Thurs - Sun
PRICE RANGE: $$
NEIGHBORHOOD: Downtown
Full service cut-to-order cheese counter and eatery. Try the grilled cheese and tomato soup – it's the best. The grilled cheese sandwich is expertly browned and the cheeses used (German Butterkase & 2 different aged cheddars) make all the difference. Other favorites like Mac & cheese and Ham melt.

EGGSLUT
Grand Central Market
317 S Broadway, Los Angeles, 213-625-0292
www.eggslut.com
CUISINE: Breakfast / Brunch
DRINKS: No Booze
SERVING: 8 a.m. – 4 p.m.
PRICE RANGE: $
NEIGHBORHOOD: Downtown
It's all about eggs. Eggs served every way imaginable but you should try "The Slut" – a dish that's like mashed potatoes in a jar but with a poached egg

("coddled" egg, actually) and buttered toast for dipping. The Eggslut Sandwich is definitely the best egg sandwich in all of California. Try to avoid the weekends. Wait times average an hour.

ENGINE CO. NO. 28
644 S Figueroa St., Los Angeles: 213-624-6996
www.engineco.com
CUISINE: American
DRINKS: Full Bar
SERVING: Breakfast/ Lunch/ Dinner (on weekends lunch/ dinner only)
PRICE RANGE: $$
Comfort food at its best. A restored actual fire station that churns out LA's best meatloaf, fried chicken and lemonade, all in an elegant atmosphere with great service.

THE FACTORY KITCHEN
1300 Factory Pl, Los Angeles, 213-996-6000
www.thefactorykitchen.com
CUISINE: Italian

DRINKS: Full Bar
SERVING: Lunch & Dinner; Dinner only on Sat & Sun
PRICE RANGE: $$$
NEIGHBORHOOD: Downtown
Northern Italian eatery that is all about the pasta. My Favorites: Agnolotti stuffed with veal-beef mixture and Mandilli de seta. Great selection of meat dishes but vegetarian options available. Nice selection of Italian desserts.

FOUND OYSTER
4880 Fountain Ave, Los Angeles, 323) 486-7920
www.foundoyster.com
CUISINE: Seafood
DRINKS: Beer & Wine Only
SERVING: Dinner 4-11 weekdays, Sat & Sun noon to 11 pm; Closed Mondays
PRICE RANGE: $$

NEIGHBORHOOD: East Hollywood
Small, comfortable eatery specializing in oysters (raw, fried, broiled—I like the broiled—don't see them that often) and other seafood specialties like Scallop tostada; Grilled leeks; Tasty clam chowder and the lobster roll makes you feel like you're (almost) on Cape Cod. No reservations. Walk-ins only.

GISH BAC
4163 W Washington Blvd, Los Angeles, 323-737-5050
www.gishbac.com

CUISINE: Mexican / Oaxacan
DRINKS: No Booze
SERVING: Breakfast, Lunch, & Dinner
PRICE RANGE: $$
NEIGHBORHOOD: Arlington Heights / Central L.A.
Family-owned simple but quaint Mexican eatery specializing in authentic Oaxacan dishes. Favorites: Barbacoa Enchilada and Mole Negro (which is among the best mole I've ever had outside Mexico). Mexican sodas, juices, and shakes.

GRAND CENTRAL MARKET
317 S. Broadway, Los Angeles: 213-624-2378
www.grandcentralsquare.com
CUISINE: Mexican/ Grocery
DRINKS: Beer/ Wine
SERVING: Lunch/ Dinner
PRICE RANGE: $
Huge indoor bazaar of Central and South American vendors. Get fresh tortillas, huge Mexican papayas and tasty tortas.

HORSE THIEF BBQ
Grand Central Market
324 S Hill St, Los Angeles, 213-625-0341
www.horsethiefbbq.com
CUISINE: Barbeque
DRINKS: Beer & Wine
SERVING: Lunch Mon – Tues, Lunch & Dinner Wed - Sun
PRICE RANGE: $$
NEIGHBORHOOD: Downtown

Casual eatery offering Texas-style slow-smoked barbecue (smoked for 15 hours). They sell it by the quarter-pound. Order from the counter and eat at long communal tables—the patio is the best. Craft beers you can get from a walk-up counter. My Favorites: Brisket sandwich and Pulled Pork sandwich.

HOWLIN' RAY'S
Far East Plaza
727 N Broadway, Los Angeles, 213-935-8399
www.howlinrays.com
CUISINE: Nashville-style Hot Chicken
DRINKS: No Booze
SERVING: Lunch & Dinner; Closed Mondays
PRICE RANGE: S$
NEIGHBORHOOD: Chinatown

Tiny counter-only eatery offering Nashville-style hot chicken and hearty sides. Favorites: Any of the Hot Chicken combos; Chicken & Waffles and Fried chicken sandwich. Chicken comes in several levels of heat, from no heat to Howlin'. Very busy on weekends, often an hour and half wait. Smart people come an hour before opening to insure getting served expeditiously.

JOY
5100 York Blvd, Los Angeles, 323-999-7642
www.joyonyork.com
CUISINE: Taiwanese / Chinese
DRINKS: Beer & Wine Only
SERVING: Lunch & Dinner
PRICE RANGE: $$
NEIGHBORHOOD: Highland Park
Not really Downtown, but I have to put this popular hip eatery serving Taiwanese classics somewhere.

Order at the counter and then grab a table. You'll get a number. When your chow is ready, you'll get it. Favorites: Clam shell bun w/pork belly and Slack Season Noodles (chicken & pork broth, minced pork, garlic & shrimp). Usually a 20-minute wait, but oh my, well worth it.

KANG HODONG BAEKJEONG
3465 W 6th St, Los Angeles, 213-384-9678
www.kijung.com
CUISINE: Korean / BBQ
DRINKS: Beer & Wine Only
SERVING: Lunch & Dinner
PRICE RANGE: $$
NEIGHBORHOOD: Downtown/Koreatown
Popular Korean BBQ joint - there's almost always a line but well worth the wait. Maybe the best Korean BBQ in L.A. My Favorites: Pork combo with Doenjang Chigae. Set menu or a la carte options.

LANGER'S DELI
704 S Alvarado St, Los Angeles, 213-483-8050
www.langersdeli.com
CUISINE: Delis / Sandwiches
DRINKS: Beer & Wine Only
SERVING: Lunch, Dinner
PRICE RANGE: S$
NEIGHBORHOOD: Westlake; Downtown
This is one of LA's most popular delis. Menu includes typical deli fare like corned beef and pastrami sandwiches but their bakery items are the best. Known as serving the World's Best Pastrami sandwich, and it's no wonder. It's their gold

standard—pastrami piled high on double-baked rye bread. Extensive deli menu. Closed Sundays.

M.GEORGINA
777 Alameda St, Los Angeles, 213-334-4113
www.mgeorgina.com
CUISINE: American (New)
DRINKS: Full Bar
SERVING: Opens for happy hour at 3:30 before dinner at 5; Closed Mondays
PRICE RANGE: $$$
NEIGHBORHOOD: Downtown
A bright airy room in the day (when, oddly, it's not open) that gets cozy and intimate at night, this popular dinner spot (especially on weekends, so come during the week) offering American fare with a twist. Some of the best dishes come from the wood-burning oven. Combine one of those with one of their great pastas and you have got a winner. Menu picks: Kobocha/onion tempura and Squid ink pita. Delicious desserts.

MA'AM SIR
4330 Sunset Blvd, Los Angeles, 323-741-8371
www.maamsirla.com
CUISINE: Filipino
DRINKS: Full Bar
SERVING: Dinner
PRICE RANGE: $$
NEIGHBORHOOD: Silver Lake
Funky little eatery serving Filipino cuisine. Favorites: Longganisa Burger and Crispy Pork Lechon. Creative cocktails.

MAJORDOMO
1725 Naud St, Los Angeles, 323-545-4880
https://www.majordomo.la
CUISINE: Korean / Seafood
DRINKS: Full bar
SERVING: Dinner Tues-Sat; closed Sun & Mon
PRICE RANGE: $$$$

NEIGHBORHOOD: Chinatown
In this huge concrete hall sequestered in an industrial courtyard you'll find David Chang's hotspot. Lots of wood paneling and shelving help to lessen the feeling you're in a concrete Soviet Era bunker. The Spartan tables and chairs seem softened just by the elegant wine glasses topping every table. Picks: Peppers stuffed with Benton sausage & the Spicy lamb make good starters; also the smoked cabbage with brown butter; Excellent main courses are the Crispy pork belly; 45-day dry-aged Holstein rib eye. Menu changes daily, so there's always something new.

MARISCOS JALISCO
3040 E Olympic Blvd, Los Angeles, 323-528-6701
http://mariscos-jalisco.cafes-world.com/
CUISINE: Mexican
DRINKS: No Booze
SERVING: 9 a.m. – 6 p.m.

PRICE RANGE: $
NEIGHBORHOOD: Boyle Heights
No-frills Mexican food truck featuring cold seafood dishes. Favorites: Fried Shrimp Tacos and Shrimp Tostada.

NIGHT + MARKET SONG
3322 W Sunset Blvd, Los Angeles, 323-665-5899
Night + Market, 9043 Sunset Blvd, West Hollywood, 310-275-9724.
www.nightmarketsong.com
CUISINE: Thai
DRINKS: Beer & Wine
SERVING: Lunch & Dinner; Dinner only on Sat; closed Sun
PRICE RANGE: $$
NEIGHBORHOOD: Silver Lake
Popular Thai eatery with an impressive menu. No reservations. My Favorites: Coconut glazed pork

satay; Grapow Khai Dao; Thai Boxing Chicken (served with sticky rice).

NIGHTSHADE
923 E 3rd St, Ste 109, Los Angeles, 213-626-8888
www.nightshadela.com
CUISINE: Asian Fusion
DRINKS: Full Bar
SERVING: Dinner; Closed Mondays
PRICE RANGE: $$$
NEIGHBORHOOD: Arts District, Downtown
Seasonal Asian-Californian cuisine. Favorites: Lasagna with pork ragu and Prawn toast with Cantonese curry. Their short ribs are amazing but go early as they sell out.

OTIUM
Broad Museum
222 S Hope St, Los Angeles, 213-935-8500
www.otiumla.com
CUISINE: American (New)
DRINKS: Full Bar
SERVING: Lunch & Dinner; closed Mon
PRICE RANGE: $$$
NEIGHBORHOOD: Downtown
Upscale eatery with a creative menu located in the exciting Broad Museum. My Favorites: Rock Shrimp Lettuce Wraps; Hoe Cake and Crispy Pork Belly. Try the Bread Pudding French Toast served with small pieces of fried chicken and caramelized banana, all over a campfire.

PACIFIC DINING CAR
1310 West 6th St, Los Angeles: 213-483-6000
www.pacificdiningcar.com
CUISINE: Steakhouse

DRINKS: Full Bar
SERVING: Breakfast/ Lunch/ Dinner/ Late Night
PRICE RANGE: $$$$
NEIGHBORHOOD: Downtown

Since 1921 this unique spot has been a fixture on the L.A. dining scene. Originally started in a rail car Downtown, Pacific Dining Car has been owned and operated by the same family ever since. (The Santa Monica location opened in 1990.) They serve prime aged corn-fed beef, as well as seafood, veal and other items for non-beef eaters. If you ever wondered what it was like to ride in a robber baron's private rail car, get your butt over here and sink into their plush velvet seats and admire the highly polished rich wood paneling. Heavy draperies, good art on the walls, fine service in an ultra-plush atmosphere. Since they're open 24 hours, this is also a good place to catch breakfast or swing by for a late-night snack or full meal after hitting the town. Favorites: for b'fast, I like the sautéed Cinnamon Apples served with their house-made sausage that's to die for; for lunch I usually get the Baseball Steak (a thick cut aged top sirloin you don't see very often), the 8 oz, not the bigger 16 oz—that's too much for lunch; at dinner, I opt for the Warm Spinach Salad and the Prime New York Strip. If it's late night (which it very often is), I jump on the Eggs Sardou or the Huevos Rancheros. Ask for the breakfast menu any time, day or night, for a more affordable and quite delicious menu.

THE PALM
1100 S Flower St, Los Angeles, 213-763-4600
www.thepalm.com

CUISINE: Steakhouse
DRINKS: Full Bar
SERVING: Lunch & Dinner; Dinner only Sat & Sun
PRICE RANGE: $$$
NEIGHBORHOOD: Downtown
Downtown L.A.'s outpost of the classic New York chain known as the "granddaddy of steakhouses." Classy dining experience with the biggest lobsters west of the Mississippi. Filets are infamous and the Lobster Mac 'n Cheese is a must.

PAPA CRISTO'S
2771 W. Pico Blvd., Los Angeles: 323-737-2970
www.papacristos.com
WEB SITE DOWN AT PRESS TIME
CUISINE: Greek
DRINKS: Beer and wine
SERVING: Tues – Sat lunch and dinner, Sun lunch, Mon closed
PRICE RANGE: $$

NEIGHBORHOOD: South LA
Run by the same family since 1948, here you'll get good Greek food in what, besides being a tavern, is also a gourmet market and bakery (don't leave without some baklava). Every Thursday they have specials and belly dancers entertain. (Or not. Remember what Noel Coward said about them in his song "Nina"? "Forever wiggling their guts! It drives me absolutely nuts!")

PARK'S BBQ
955 S Vermont Ave, Los Angeles, 213-380-1717
www.parksbbq.com
CUISINE: Korean / BBQ
DRINKS: Full Bar
SERVING: Lunch & Dinner
PRICE RANGE: $$$
NEIGHBORHOOD: Downtown/Koreatown
Popular Korean BBQ eatery (the original one is in Seoul) with an impressive selection of juicy meats. Simple décor and it's all about the meat from brisket to boneless short rib. It's right up there with the best of them in this category.

RED HERRING
770 S Grand Ave, Los Angeles, 213-375-3290
www.redherringla.com
CUISINE: International / French / Middle East
DRINKS: Full Bar
SERVING: Lunch & Dinner, Brunch
PRICE RANGE: $$
NEIGHBORHOOD: Downtown
You can't be downtrodden for long when you walk into this bright cheery room with its uplifting pastels. Though its bills itself as a Los Angeles home for "New American Comfort Food," apart from its location here in downtown L.A., there seems to be very little 'American' about it, with dishes inspired from places as far apart as Mexico to Beirut. Menu picks: Chicken & Waffles (for brunch), but it's really fried quail stuffed with homemade chicken maple sage sausage) and Duck Confit. Interesting dishes like

"braised eggs," Crispy Smoked Potato. Popular brunch destination. Indoor & outdoor seating.

REDBIRD
114 E 2nd St, Los Angeles, 213-788-1191
www.redbird.la
CUISINE: American (New)
DRINKS: Full Bar
SERVING: Dinner, Lunch on Sat & Sun
PRICE RANGE: $$$
NEIGHBORHOOD: Downtown
Located in a beautiful historical building (formerly the Cathedral of St. Vibiana, once the seat of the Catholic Archdiocese, that suffered damage in the 1994 earthquake), this eatery (located in the former rectory) offers a great upscale dining experience. Though the building is historic, the design is not—a very modern look focused on a visually compelling courtyard. My Favorites: Day boat scallops; Rack of Red Wattle Pork; Chicken pot pie. Nice wine selection – sommelier on site. Creative desserts like Mexican chocolate with canela and passion fruit. Good brunch spot.

REPUBLIQUE
624 S La Brea Ave, Los Angeles, 310-362-6115
www.republiquela.com
CUISINE: French
DRINKS: Full Bar
SERVING: Lunch & Dinner
PRICE RANGE: $$
NEIGHBORHOOD: Downtown
Beautifully designed French-inspired eatery. My Favorites: Mafaldine and Spinach Cavatelli. Fabulous pastry. A must-try for brunch.

ROSSOBLU
1124 San Julian St, Los Angeles, 213-749-1099
www.rossoblula.com
CUISINE: Italian
DRINKS: Full Bar
SERVING: Dinner, Lunch & Dinner on Sundays
PRICE RANGE: $$$
NEIGHBORHOOD: Downtown
Upscale Bolognese-inspired eatery featuring handmade pastas. Favorites: Bolognese and Lamb shank. Impressive wine list. Reservations recommended.

SARITA'S PUPUSERIA
Grand Central Market
317 S Broadway, Ste E-5, 213-626-6320
www.grandcentralmarket.com/vendors/32/saritas-pupuseria
CUISINE: Salvadorian
DRINKS: No Booze
SERVING: Lunch & Dinner
PRICE RANGE: $
NEIGHBORHOOD: Downtown
Casual eatery offering El Salvador cuisine. There's usually a line but worth the wait. Favorite: Pork and Chorizo pupusas.

SONORATOWN
208 E 8th St, Los Angeles, 213-628-3710
www.sonoratown.com
CUISINE: Tacos
DRINKS: No Booze
SERVING: Lunch & Dinner
PRICE RANGE: $
NEIGHBORHOOD: Downtown
Casual eatery serving Northern Mexican–style cuisine. Known for their handmade flour tortillas. Favorites: Tacos, tacos, and tacos (Steak, Chicken, Tripe, and Pork). Small place with indoor and outdoor seating.

STICKY RICE
Grand Central Market
317 S Broadway, Ste C-4-5, Los Angeles, 213-621-2865
www.stickyricegcm.com

CUISINE: Thai
DRINKS: No Booze
SERVING: Lunch & Dinner
PRICE RANGE: $$
NEIGHBORHOOD: Downtown
Popular eatery serving fresh authentic Thai dishes from one of the smallest kitchens I've ever seen. Try to get a seat at the counter so you can watch how efficiently they are working. My Favorites: Pad Kee Mau; Gai Yang (tart Thai BBQ chicken); Spicy Basil Chicken and jasmine rice. Delicious pastries.

TACOCS TUMBRAS A TOMAS
Grand Central Market
317 S Broadway, Los Angeles, 213-620-1071
www.grandcentralsquare.com/
CUISINE: Mexican
DRINKS: No Booze
SERVING: 9 a.m. – 6 p.m.
PRICE RANGE: $
NEIGHBORHOOD: Downtown
Popular eatery for the food and the price. Portions are huge. You'll take half of what you order here home with you. My Favorites: Carnitas taco and Carne aside tostada.

TSUBAKI
1356 Allison Ave, Los Angeles, 213-900-4900
www.tsubakila.com
CUISINE: Japanese / Izakaya
DRINKS: Beer & Wine Only
SERVING: Dinner
PRICE RANGE: $$$
NEIGHBORHOOD: Echo Park
Informal tavern atmosphere serving classic izakaya. Favorites: 48-hour short rib and Scallops. Make a reservation – gets crowded on weekends. Save room for Green tea soft serve.

UMAMIBURGER
852 S. Broadway, Los Angeles: 213-413-8626
www.umami.com/umamicatessen

CUISINE: Delis
DRINKS: Full bar
SERVING: Daily lunch and dinner
PRICE RANGE: $$
NEIGHBORHOOD: Downtown

In the movie business they have a term, "high-concept," and that could easily be applied to this place. I dare you to wander into this wildly creative mashup of a food place and not be seduced by one of the offerings. It's got an **Umami Burger** section (try to Truffle Burger with homemade truffle cheese and a truffle glaze), a coffee shop, a New York-style deli with all the good things that implies, a donut shop, and best of all, **Pigg**, Chris Cosentino's place where the focus is on all things pork: delectable hams, charcuteries, terrines and salumi. (They spell it with an ! in it, like P!GG.)

WOODSPOON

107 W 9th St, Los Angeles: 213-629-1765
www.woodspoonla.com
CUISINE: Brazilian
DRINKS: Beer/ Wine
SERVING: Lunch/ Dinner (closed Sundays and Mondays)
PRICE RANGE: $$
NEIGHBORHOOD: Downtown

Doesn't look like much on the outside, but you'll flip over the Brazilian-inspired dishes that are different from what most American restaurants serve as "Brazilian." Sure, you'll see the usual rice, beans and plantains, but it's low-key Brazilian comfort food of the highest order. Order the chicken pot pie, the carne de panela or the tilapia platter. Drink sangria with your dinner.

WURSTKÜCHE
800 E. 3rd St., Los Angeles: 213-687-4444
www.wurstkuche.com
CUISINE: Hot dogs / German / Gastropub
DRINKS: Beer and wine
SERVING: Daily lunch and dinner
PRICE RANGE: $$
NEIGHBORHOOD: Downtown
Sort of an upmarket beer hall reimagined. In addition to the standard wursts, they offer unusual takes on hot dogs and sausages (like one that mixes rabbit, veal and pork). Get some Belgian fries and a beer (24 imported beers on tap), and you're all set. This is a big barn of a place, formerly an industrial printing plant. They attract a big crowd, so the earlier you go,

the better. A DJ cranks out electronica when things get going. (Has a location in Venice as well.)

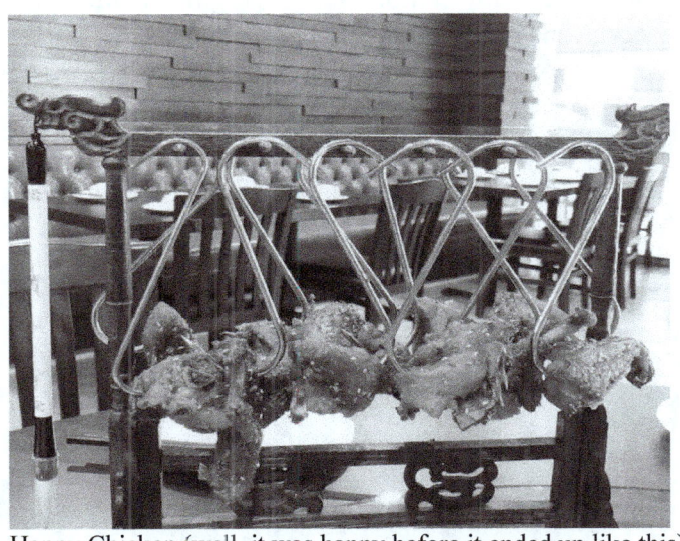

Happy Chicken (well, it was happy before it ended up like this). Maybe 'Tasty Chicken' works better, because it's certainly that.

XIANG LA HUI
621 W Main St, Alhambra, 626-703-4165
https://xiang-la-hui.business.site
CUISINE: Szechuan / Sichuan
DRINKS: No Booze
SERVING: Lunch & Dinner
PRICE RANGE: $$
NEIGHBORHOOD: Alhambra
A bit out of town, about 8 miles from Downtown, so I will put it there in my listings. But it's important. Szechuan eatery offering a very good menu of this spicy cuisine (come early as many of the best dishes

sell out). Has one of those "photo menus" common to Chinese eateries, but the food is not typical, much better than the menu would have you think. Favorites: Toothpick Cumin Lamb; Chong Qing fried chicken. Reservations recommended.

YXTA COCINA MEXICANA
601 S Central Ave., Los Angeles, 213-596-5579
www.yxta.net
CUISINE: Mexican
DRINKS: Beer and wine
SERVING: Lunch Mon-Fri; dinner Mon-Sat; closed Sun
PRICE RANGE: $$
NEIGHBORHOOD: Downtown
The Mexican food you get here is authentic. Expect homemade tortillas, fresh guacamole, tortas, carnitas slow-cooked the right way, enchiladas de mole, and

chile rellenos. They also have their own twists on some classics—tostadas with sashimi-grade tuna, sweet shrimp taquitos, and salmon in cilantro pesto, by way of examples. They serve Salmon Creek natural pork and Jidori free range chicken, something you won't find in other Mexican joints in town.

Chapter 4
SANTA MONICA & VENICE

DID YOU FIND AN INTERESTING PLACE?
If you discover a place you think I should check out on my next visit, drop me a line, will you? I'll mention your name if I end up listing it.
andrewdelaplaine@mac.com

Venice and Santa Monica weren't always a foodie paradise. But the times, they have a-changed. One thing, though, that's really nice about Venice: it's not outrageously priced the way so many other restaurants in L.A. are. The eateries here price their menu items for locals who live here. You share the benefits.

ARTHUR J
903 Manhattan Ave, Manhattan Beach, 310-878-9620
www.thearthurj.com
CUISINE: Steakhouse

DRINKS: Full Bar
SERVING: Dinner
PRICE RANGE: $$$$
NEIGHBORHOOD: Manhattan Beach

This is a bit south of Santa Monica / Venice, but worth the trip. Upscale, retro-inspired eatery for steak lovers. No white tablecloths here (part of their "retro" look), but still the mood is upscale, maybe because the steaks are just so damn good. Impressive variety of meats from ribeye to filet mignon. Regulars (well, the regulars with fat wallets) order the 60-day aged tomahawk steak. Forget everything else on the menu *except* the steaks. They start you off with those old-fashioned Parker House rolls which you simply can't resist. Why are they so good? Maybe it's the deviled ham that comes with them. Once you spread a little of that on these rolls, they're irresistible. Classic cocktails. Save room for the "cake of the month." Reservations recommended.

CAFÉ DEL REY
4451 Admiralty Way, Marina Del Rey: 310-823-6395
www.cafedelreymarina.com
CUISINE: American/ Mediterranean
DRINKS: Full Bar
SERVING: Lunch/ Dinner
PRICE RANGE: $$$
Gaze out over the marina and allow your mind to drift lazily like the boats against the docks as you savor the fresh and tantalizing fare Executive Chef Niederkorn serves up daily. Only twenty minutes from the harried rush of LAX, Café Del Rey transports diners from the bustle of humanity to the calm oasis of a foreign seaside town. Chef Niederkorn presents elegantly prepared and simply adorned seafood dishes that shine by their own freshness and flavor. The Black Spaghetti is made with prawns, calamari, lobster, and bay scallops; and the Mediterranean Meatloaf is taken to another level by a topping of black truffle gravy.

CASA ADO
12 Washington Ave, Marina Del Rey, 310-577-2589
www.casaado.com
CUISINE: Italian / Pizza
DRINKS: Full Bar
SERVING: Dinner nightly, Lunch on Sat. & Sun.
PRICE RANGE: $$
NEIGHBORHOOD: Marina del Rey
Upscale Italian joint serving up great pastas on a large and well-balanced menu featuring all the great specialties. My Favorites: Pan sautéed clams &

mussels; Dover Sole; Beet pasta. Their tiramisu is worth trying. Piano player in the dining area.

CASSIA
1314 Seventh St (at Arizona Ave), Santa Monica, 310-393-6699
www.cassiala.com
CUISINE: Singaporean / Vietnamese / Seafood
DRINKS: Full Bar
SERVING: Dinner;
PRICE RANGE: $$$
NEIGHBORHOOD: Santa Monica
Southeast Asian brasserie specializing in Vietnamese, Singaporean, and Chinese cuisines set in a very open, high-ceilinged airy space. You can see through to the kitchen beyond the raw bar and wood grill. There's outside seating on the street. Besides the spectacular food served here, you'll find a welcoming attitude from the staff and a complete lack of pretension, something you can't say about many other places in L.A. My Favorites: Spicy lamb breast grilled is succulent and mouthwatering; interesting charcuterie platters that very much reflect the Asian influences on display here (think Vietnamese pork meatloaf and candied bacon rendered Singapore style); Vietnamese "Sunbathing" Prawns and Grilled Pig's Tail. Great desserts like the Vietnamese Coffee Pudding.

FATHER'S OFFICE
1018 Montana Ave, Santa Monica, 310-736-2224
www.fathersoffice.com
CUISINE: Burgers/American (New)
DRINKS: Beer & Wine
SERVING: Dinner, Lunch on Sat & Sun
PRICE RANGE: $$
NEIGHBORHOOD: Santa Monica

Known for their creative dry-aged burgers and sweet potato fries. Nice selection of beers. Crowded on weekend nights. If you ask for ketchup, you'll get "that look."

FELIX TRATTORIA
1023 Abbot Kinney Blvd, Los Angeles, 424-387-8622
www.felixla.com
CUISINE: Italian

DRINKS: Full Bar
SERVING: Dinner
PRICE RANGE: $$$
NEIGHBORHOOD: Venice

Upscale eatery serving traditional Italian fare. Pastas made right before your eyes. Branzino roasted to perfection and Focaccia that melts in your mouth. Favorites: Pizzas (all of them); the Orecchiette (not sure what they do to the sausage in this dish, but it's spectacular); and Pork meatballs. Order family style and you'll have more than enough food. Reservations needed.

GJELINA

1429 Abbot Kinney Blvd., Venice: 310-450-1429
www.gjelina.com
CUISINE: American / Nouveau-peasant
DRINKS: beer / wine
SERVING: lunch / dinner / brunch (weekends they open at 9 a.m., brunch till 3); reservations only for parties of 6 or more.

This spot has a national reputation, and attracts such celebs as Chef Gordon Ramsay and Robert Downey, Jr., who have chaffed at the "no substitutions" policy. This is the hardest place to get a table, but you can try to squeeze in early. I'm a big fan of the way they handle their vegetable specialties: braised green garbanzos with soffrito, feta, mint and pomegranate; grilled romano beans with confit cherry tomato & za'atar; seared okra with black olive, tomato, pinenut and mint; grilled rapini with garlic, chili and vinegar; grilled radicchio with balsamic and sea salt; roasted thumbelina carrots with orange, sesame, cilantro &

yogurt; wood roasted cauliflower with garlic, chili & vinegar.

GJUSTA
320 Sunset Ave, Los Angeles, 310-314-0320
www.gjusta.com
CUISINE: Café/Deli
DRINKS: No Booze
SERVING: Breakfast, Lunch & Dinner
PRICE RANGE: $$
NEIGHBORHOOD: Venice
Rustic café with a large creative menu offering a casual Venice experience. (Expect a few scruffy beach bums.) My Favorites: Reuben sandwich and Short rib banh mi. Bakery counter in front with an inviting selection of baked breads and sweets. Take a number and wait. You won't be disappointed.

HINOKI & THE BIRD
10 W Century Dr, Los Angeles, 310-552-1200
www.hinokiandthebird.com
CUISINE: American (New)
DRINKS: Full Bar
SERVING: Lunch & Dinner – Tues – Fri, Lunch only on Mon, Dinner only on Sat; Closed Sun
PRICE RANGE: $$$
NEIGHBORHOOD: Century City
Lively eatery that melds California cuisine with a strong Asian influence. There's a gorgeous terrace that features a wall with living plants climbing up it. My Favorites: Wild Boar Ribs and Roast suckling pig. Creative cocktails. Nice wine list.

JODY MARONI'S SAUSAGE KINGDOM
2011 Ocean Front Walk, 310-822-5639
www.jodymaroni.com
Though Jody has several locations in Greater L.A., this is the original one. Jody is renowned in "sausage circles" as one of the best artisans of the craft. He was the originator of upmarket chicken sausages, which are now seen all over the country. Here you can get some of the most creative sausages you've ever seen. There's one type made with jalapenos, corn and fresh lime. Another with oranges, fennel and wine. They're all bursting with flavor.

KATO RESTAURANT
11925 Santa Monica Blvd, Los Angeles, 424-535-3041
www.katorestaurant.com
CUISINE: Japanese / Taiwanese
DRINKS: No Booze / BYOB
SERVING: Dinner; Closed Mon & Sun
PRICE RANGE: $$$$
NEIGHBORHOOD: Sawtelle
Located in a sad-sack strip-mall with a minimalist décor (OK—no décor at all) but still very welcoming. While the place looks like it ought to be cheap, cheap, cheap, it's anything but. It even has a Michelin star. Known for their fresh seafood 9-course tasting menu. An extended menu with more courses is available with dishes like Tuna Toast, Spiny Lobster, Crab, Turbot and Sablefish. BYOB (no corkage fee).

LARRY'S
24 Windward Ave., Venice: 310-399-2700

www.larrysvenice.com
CUISINE: Caribbean / Gastropub
DRINKS: beer / wine
SERVING: Lunch / Dinner
Near the colorful Venice boardwalk you'll find this place carrying 24 draft beers. Seared king scallops are good, not to mention the lamb burger. Named after local artist Larry Bell.

PACIFIC DINING CAR
http://www.pacificdiningcar.com/
2700 Wilshire Blvd, Santa Monica, 310-453-4000
CUISINE: Steakhouse
DRINKS: Full bar
SERVING: 24-hours
PRICE RANGE: $$$-$$$$
NEIGHBORHOOD: Santa Monica
Since 1921 this unique spot has been a fixture on the L.A. dining scene. Originally started in a rail car Downtown, Pacific Dining Car has been owned and

operated by the same family ever since. (The Santa Monica location opened in 1990.) They serve prime aged corn-fed beef, as well as seafood, veal and other items for non-beef eaters. If you ever wondered what it was like to ride in a robber baron's private rail car, get your butt over here and sink into their plush velvet seats and admire the highly polished rich wood paneling. Heavy draperies, good art on the walls, fine service in an ultra-plush atmosphere. Since they're open 24 hours, this is also a good place to catch breakfast or swing by for a late-night snack or full meal after hitting the town. Favorites: for b'fast, I like the sautéed Cinnamon Apples served with their house-made sausage that's to die for; for lunch I usually get the Baseball Steak (a thick cut aged top sirloin you don't see very often), the 8 oz, not the bigger 16 oz—that's too much for lunch; at dinner, I opt for the Warm Spinach Salad and the Prime New York Strip. If it's late night (which it very often is), I jump on the Eggs Sardou or the Huevos Rancheros.

THE PENTHOUSE
AT THE HUNTLEY HOTEL
1111 Second St, Santa Monica, 310-393-8080
www.thehuntleyhotel.com
CUISINE: Mediterranean / Greek / American
DRINKS: Full Bar
SERVING: B'fast; Lunch; Dinner
PRICE RANGE: $$$
NEIGHBORHOOD: Beverly Hills
Not your typical hotel eatery. This one boasts incredible views of the sky, coastline and mountains in the distance from the 18th floor of the Huntley.

Lots of windows, elegantly designed. Offers a so-so menu of Mediterranean fare tilting toward Greece, even though if you took the few Greek dishes off the menu, it would be completely American. You're here for the view, not the food. Great spot for breakfast or brunch so you can take in the spectacular views. At the same time, it's romantic at night. My Favorites: Orzo pasta with braised short ribs; Grilled Haloumi cheese; Angus Flat Iron Steak; Banana Foster French toast.

ONDA
Proper Hotel
700 Wilshire Blvd, Santa Monica, 310-620-9917
www.onda.la
CUISINE: Mexican

DRINKS: Full Bar
SERVING: Dinner nightly from 5
PRICE RANGE: $$$
NEIGHBORHOOD: Santa Monica

People are flocking to this long narrow room that's been carved out of the Proper Hotel in Santa Monica that's been transformed into an upscale eatery offering a menu of classic Mexican fare with a seafood focus. I've always had a problem wrapping my head around the concept of "upscale Mexican food." As in: how could Mexican food ever be "upscale"? When you're dealing with what is essentially peasant food, it always seems to me to be best at its most simple. Its most basic. Here, however, they bring a few twists that really does elevate the cuisine. An emphasis on high-quality ingredients also makes a difference. (Favorites: Inside Out Turkey Quesadilla and Fish Hiding in Kelp (this is corn masa-battered kelp, anchovies and lemon fritto misto with salsa verde. Unusual but tasty desserts.

PASJOLI
2732 Main St, Santa Monica, 424-330-0020
www.pasjoli.com
CUISINE: French
DRINKS: Full Bar
SERVING: Dinner
PRICE RANGE: $$$$
NEIGHBORHOOD: Santa Monica
Upscale Parisian bistro offering a menu a step above traditional French classics in a room with exposed overhead beams, a/c ductwork to give it a little "industrial" feel. There's seating at the bar as well. Favorites: Rack of Lamb and Sole meuniere. The pressed duck (for 2) is served tableside, and it's spectacular. Impressive list of French wines and cocktails. Reservations recommended.

PONO BURGER
829 Broadway, Santa Monica, 310-584-7005

www.ponoburger.com
CUISINE: Burgers/American (New)
DRINKS: Beer & Wine
SERVING: Lunch & Dinner
PRICE RANGE: $$
NEIGHBORHOOD: Santa Monica

Hawaiian burger eatery with a limited menu but everything is good. The burgers here feature unusual spices that give them a distinctively creative burst of flavor you haven't experienced before. My Favorites: Fig Burger and Sassy Wahine burger. Gluten free options. Free underground parking.

SOCALO
1920 Santa Monica Blvd, 310-451-1655
www.socalo.com
CUISINE: Mexican
DRINKS: Full Bar
SERVING: Breakfast, Lunch, & Dinner
PRICE RANGE: $$
NEIGHBORHOOD: Santa Monica

Located in Santa Monica's **Gateway Hotel**, this eatery offers all day dining with a Mexican pub-style atmosphere. Order at the counter, then find your own seat, or even better, sit at the bar and sip margaritas while you wait. (They're good, trust me.) This place is tucked away on the eastern side of Santa Monica, so you've got a little distance between you and the surfers and tourists at the other end of town. Office workers np in here for a quick lunch. Locals flock here for an inexpensive dinner in a fun atmosphere. You should, too. Favorites: Salmon poke; Mexicali Ceviche NW; excellent Burritos.

SUNNY SPOT
822 Washington Blvd., Venice: 310-448-8884
www.sunnyspotvenice.com
CUISINE: Caribbean
DRINKS: beer / wine
SERVING: dinner
Start with the jumbo shrimp fried with the heads on, followed by the Jamaican roasted pork.

THE TASTING KITCHEN
1633 Abbot Kinney Blvd., Venice: 310-392-6644
www.thetastingkitchen.com
CUISINE: Italian
DRINKS: full bar
SERVING: dinner weeknights from 6; brunch from 10:30 weekends
One of the best places for brunch (and there are several other good options besides this one). You have to like the large communal tables here. Chances are some big-time producer is sitting next to you. But

for dinner, try the bacon-wrapped scallops; their excellent selection of cheeses makes a charcuterie board a good bet here.

TEDDYS RED TACOS
46 Windward Ave, Venice, 323-495-9654
www.teddysredtacos.com
CUISINE: Tacos / Food Truck
DRINKS: No Booze
SERVING: Lunch & Dinner
PRICE RANGE: $

NEIGHBORHOOD: Venice
Taco food truck that specializes in beef, but they do offer veggie tacos. Three categories: Taco, quesadilla and tostada. Inside and outdoor seating.

Chapter 5
NIGHTLIFE

I'm just starting to add a nightlife section to L.A., so bear with me. I keep going out every time I'm there, so I might as well start sharing, right? Any spots you particularly like, let me know and I'll check them out on my next visit. I've been putting this off, but need to do it. So help me if you can.

DEATH & CO.
818 E 3rd St, Los Angeles, No Phone
www.deathandcompany.com
NEIGHBORHOOD: Arts District, Downtown
Popular bar with locations in New York and Denver. Standing room only on weekends in this underground space tucked away from prying crowds. Actually, 'Standing Room' is what they call the bar out front. Where you want to be is in the back, where there's a more intimate cocktail lounge with low lighting, a New York feel and bartenders who know how to make quality drinks. Cocktail menu is quite impressive with unusual ingredients. One of L.A.'s top hot spots.

INDEX

A

ALL DAY BABY, 50
American, 15, 23, 24, 26, 28, 30, 32, 36, 38, 40, 57
AMERICAN, 65, 95
American (New), 6, 10, 20, 22, 25, 32, 33, 34, 37, 43, 51, 56, 72, 77, 82, 97, 100, 108
American (Traditional), 30
AMICI, 5
ANA MARIA, 51
ANIMAL, 6
ARTHUR J, 93
Asian, 10, 23, 38, 96, 100
Asian Fusion, 76
AUBURN, 25

B

BACO MERCAT, 52
Bakery, 7, 29, 61
BAR AMÁ, 52
BAR RESTAURANT, 53
Barbeque, 68
BAVEL, 54
BELCAMPO MEAT CO., 56
BESTIA, 55
Beverly Wilshire, 20
BIRDS, 26
BLUE COW KITCHEN, 57
BOA STEAKHOUSE, 27
BON TEMPS, 58
BOTTEGA LOUIE, 59
BRAZILIAN, 89
Breakfast, 51, 61, 108

C

CAFE DEL REY, 95
Caribbean, 103, 109
CASA ADO, 95
CASSIA, 96
CECCONI'S, 27
CHATEAU MARMONT, 28
Cheese shop, 64
CHI SPACCA, 29
CHICHEN ITZA, 59
Chicken-rotisserie, 13
Chinese, 16, 70, 96
CHURCH & STATE, 60
CLARK STREET BREAD & PASTRY, 61
CLEMENTINE, 7, 29
CONNIE AND TED'S, 30
CRAIG'S, 30
CULINA, 8, 31
CUT, 9

D

DAIKOKUYA, 63
DAN TANA'S RESTAURANT, 31
DEATH & CO., 111
Delis, 71, 89
DESTROYER, 32
DTLA CHEESE, 64

E

E. BALDI, 9
EGGSLUT, 64
ENGINE CO. NO. 28, 65
EVELEIGH, 32

F

FACTORY KITCHEN, 65
Falafels, 15
Far East Plaza, 69
Farmers Market, 34
FATHER'S OFFICE, 97
FELIX TRATTORIA, 98
FIG & OLIVE, 33
Filipino, 73
FOUND OYSTER, 66
French, 33, 41, 47, 51, 53, 54, 81, 83, 107
French (mostly), 58
French bistro, 60
Fried Chicken Nashville-style, 11

G

Gastropub, 52, 90, 103
Gateway Hotel, 109
German, 90
GISH BAC, 67
GJELINA, 99
GJUSTA, 100
Grand Central Market, 51, 56, 64, 68, 85, 86, 87
GRAND CENTRAL MARKET, 68
Greek, 79, 104
GRILL ON THE ALLEY, 10

H

HART & THE HUNTER, 33
HERE'S LOOKING AT YOU, 34
HINOKI & THE BIRD, 10, 100
HOLLYWOOD FARMERS' MARKET, 34
Hot dogs, 42
HOTVILLE CHICKEN, 11
HOWLIN' RAY'S, 69
HUNTLEY HOTEL, 104

I

IL CIELO, 12
IL PICCOLINO, 35
Italian, 5, 8, 9, 12, 14, 19, 24, 27, 29, 31, 32, 35, 40, 41, 44, 48, 55, 59, 65, 84, 95, 98, 109
IVY, THE, 36

J

Japanese, 18, 21, 22, 38, 39, 63, 102
Japanese / Izakaya, 88
JOY, 70

K

KALI, 37
KANG HODONG BAEKJEONG, 71
KATO, 102
KATSUYA, 38
KISMET ROTISSERIE, 13
Korean, 45, 73
Korean / BBQ, 71, 80

L

La Peer Hotel, 48
LA SCALA, 14
LANGER'S DELI, 71
LARRY'S, 102
LAUREL HARDWARE, 38

M

M CAFÉ DE CHAYA, 39
M.GEORGINA, 72
MA'AM SIR, 73
MADEO, 40
MAJORDOMO, 73
MARIPOSA, 15
MARISCOS JALISCO, 74
Mediterranean, 13, 15, 33, 104
MEDITERRANEAN, 95
Mercado La Paloma, 59
Mexican, 51, 59, 63, 68, 74, 87, 92, 105, 106, 108, 109
MEXICAN, 68
Middle East, 81
Middle Eastern, 15, 54
MIZLALA, 15
MR. CHOW, 16
MUSSO & FRANK, 40

N

N/NAKA, 17
Nashville-style Hot Chicken, 69
NIGHT + MARKET SONG, 75
NIGHTSHADE, 76

O

Oaxacan, 68
OLIVETTA, 40
ONDA, 105
OTIUM, 77

P

PACIFIC DINING CAR, 77
PALM, 18, 78
PAPA CRISTO'S, 79
PARK'S BBQ, 80
PASJOLI, 107
PENTHOUSE, 104
PETIT TROIS, 41
Pigg, 89
PINK'S HOT DOGS, 42
Pizza, 19, 95
PIZZANA, 19
POLO LOUNGE, 20
PONO BURGER, 107
Proper Hotel, 105

R

RED HERRING, 81
REDBIRD, 82
REPUBLIQUE, 83
ROSSOBLU, 84

S

SALT'S CURE, 43
Salvadorian, 85
SANDWICHES, 62
SARITA'S PUPUSERIA, 85
Seafood, 66
Sichuan, 91
Singaporean, 96
SOCALO, 108
SONORATOWN, 86
SOPRANO, 44
SOUTH BEVERLY GRILL, 20
SPAGO, 22
Spanish, 52
SPOON BY H, 45
Steakhouse, 9, 10, 18, 27, 40, 79, 93
STEAKHOUSE, 77
STICKY RICE, 86
STINKING ROSE, THE, 23
SUGARFISH, 21
SUNNY SPOT, 109
Sushi, 21, 22, 46
SUSHI PARK, 46
SUSHI SASABUNE, 21
SUSHI ZO, 22
Szechuan, 91

T

TACOCS TUMBRAS A TOMAS, 87
Tacos, 86, 110
Taiwanese, 70, 102

TEDDYS RED TACOS, 110
Tex-Mex, 53
Thai, 75, 87
THE TASTING KITCHEN, 109
TOSCANOVA, 24
TROIS MEC, 47
TSUBAKI, 88

U

Umami Burger, 89
UMAMIBURGER, 88

V

Vegan, 39
Vegetarian, 33, 43
VIALE DEI ROMANI, 47
Vietnamese, 96

W

WOODSPOON, 89
WURSTKUCHE, 90

X

XIANG LA HUI, 91

Y

YXTA COCINA MEXICANA, 92

*WANT 3 **FREE** THRILLERS?*

Why, of course you do!
If you like these writers--
Vince Flynn, Brad Thor, Tom Clancy, James Patterson, David Baldacci, John Grisham, Brad Meltzer, Daniel Silva, Don DeLillo
If you like these TV series –
House of Cards, Scandal, West Wing, The Good Wife, Madam Secretary, Designated Survivor

> You'll love the **unputdownable** series about
> Jack Houston St. Clair, with political intrigue, romance,
> and loads of action and suspense.

Besides writing travel books, I've written political thrillers for many years that have delighted hundreds of thousands of readers. I want to introduce you to my work!
Send me an email and I'll send you a link where you can download the first 3 books in my bestselling series, absolutely FREE.
Mention **this book** when you email me.
andrewdelaplaine@mac.com

www.ingramcontent.com/pod-product-compliance
Lightning Source LLC
LaVergne TN
LVHW051504070426
835507LV00022B/2919